RL: 6.3

Hieroglyphs

KAREN PRICE HOSSELL

Heinemann Library
Chicago, Illinois

© 2003 Heinemann Library
a division of Reed Elsevier Inc.
Chicago, Illinois

Customer Service 888-454-2279

Visit our website at www.heinemannlibrary.com

Page layout by Vicki Fischman
Photo research by Amor Montes de Oca
Printed and bound in the United States by Lake Book
Manufacturing, Inc.

07 06 05 04 03
10 9 8 7 6 5 4 3 2 1

Library of Congress Cataloging-in-Publication Data
Price Hossell, Karen, 1957-
  Hieroglyphs / Karen Price Hossell.
    p. cm. -- (Communicating)
Summary: Discusses the hieroglyphic system of writing used
by people of the ancient Egyptian civilization along the Nile
River.
  ISBN 1-58810-485-0 (HC), 1-58810-941-0 (Pbk.)
  1. Egyptian language--Writing, Hieroglyphic--Juvenile
literature. [1.Egyptian language--Writing, Hieroglyphic.] I.
Title. II. Series.
  PJ1097 .H67 2002
  493'.111--dc21

                              2002001686

Acknowledgments
The author and publisher are grateful to the following for
permission to reproduce copyright material:
Cover photograph by Gianni Dagli Orti/Corbis
Title page Bojan Brecelj/Corbis; Illustration p.4 Tom
Szumowski/JD Originals; pp. 5, 30B, 34, 36, 37T, 40B
Gianni Dagli Orti/Corbis; Illustrations pp. 7, 10, 11 John
Fleck; p. 8T Suzanne Vlamis; pp. 8B, 20T, 30T John Elk III;
pp. 9T, 14, 26B, 29 Emily Teeter; pp. 9B, 46 Courtesy of
The Oriental Institute of the University of Chicago; p. 12
Norman Owen Tomalin/Bruce Coleman Inc.; p. 15 Emily
Teeter/The Oriental Institute of the University of Chicago;
pp. 16, 21TL, 23 Archivo Iconografico, S. A./Corbis; p. 17
Gianni Dagli Orti/Musee du Louvre, Paris/The Art Archive;
p. 18T Ludovic Maisant/Corbis; p. 18B Jay Ireland &
Georgienne Bradley/Bradleyireland.com; pp. 19T, 22, 38 E.
R. Degginger/Color Pic, Inc.; pp. 19BL, 32T H.
Rogers/TRIP; pp. 19BR, 27T, 33R Roger Wood/Corbis; p.
20B Eugene G. Schultz; p. 21TR Vanni Archive/Corbis; p.
21B Wolfgang Kaehler/Corbis; pp. 24, 35 Erich Lessing/Art
Resource; pp. 25T, 28 Sandro Vannini/Corbis; p. 25B
Jaqueline Hyde/British Museum/The Art Archive; p. 26T L.
Jackson/TRIP; p. 27B Christine Osborne Pictures; p. 31 J.C.
Carton/Bruce Coleman Inc.; pp. 32B, 33L The British
Museum/Topham/The Image Works; p. 37B Bob
Burch/Bruce Coleman Inc.; p. 39T Art Resource; p. 39B
Hulton Archive/Getty Images; p. 40T Charles & Josette
Lenars/Corbis; p. 41 Reuters NewMedia Inc./Corbis; p. 43
Nik Wheeler/Corbis

Special thanks to Dr. Emily Teeter for her help in the
preparation of this book.

About the consultant
Dr. Emily Teeter is a Research Associate and Curator of
Egyptian and Nubian Antiquities at the Oriental Institute of
the University of Chicago. She has studied Egyptian
hieroglyphs for more than 25 years. She is the co-author of
many books and articles on ancient Egyptian culture.

Some words are shown in bold,
like this. You can find out what they
mean by looking in the glossary.

Contents

Egyptian Hieroglyphs

For more than 3,000 years, a great **civilization** existed along the Nile River in the present-day country of Egypt. The organized civilization of ancient Egypt began in about 3200 B.C.E. and ended around C.E. 200 with its conversion to Christianity. While it lasted, millions of people worked, played, and worshiped along the long, winding river. They built homes to live in, temples to worship in, and **pyramids** where they buried their kings. They planted crops and built boats so they could sail up and down the Nile—the river that was, to them, the center of the world.

The Nile is the longest river in the world. It flows for 4,145 miles (6,670 kilometers) through the northeastern part of the continent of Africa. The people of ancient Egypt used the river as a highway. But it was important to them for another reason. Every summer, the Nile flooded the land on either side of the river for several miles. When the water went back down in the fall, the land was covered with a new layer of rich, black soil.

Egypt is located in northeast Africa. Temples and pyramids are found along the Nile River.

The ancient Egyptians depended on this yearly flooding and the new layer of soil it provided. Many of them were farmers who planted crops in the rich new earth. The Egyptians also built their towns near the banks of the river. Few people ever traveled more than a few miles away from the banks of the Nile, because most of the rest of Egypt is desert.

As the **culture** of ancient Egypt developed, it became more and more important to have a regular system of writing. The Egyptians created and used a special form of writing called **hieroglyphs.** This word comes from the Greek language and means "sacred sign."

Instead of the letters used in the English language, hieroglyphic writing is made up of symbols. The symbols look like people, animals, plants, and many other objects. This writing was carved into the walls of **monuments,** temples, and tombs, where the symbols provided important information. In tombs, for example, the hieroglyphs often told who was buried inside. They also included prayers to the ancient Egyptian gods and gave the dead person guidance for the **afterlife.**

The government of ancient Egypt also used writing to keep records. There were lists of who paid taxes and the items stored in warehouses. Ancient Egyptians wrote down what crops were grown and how much of each was produced, sold, stored, or traded with other countries. When they built a monument, ancient Egyptians made lists of all the building supplies they used. They kept track of workers and what jobs they did. Even the army recorded who its soldiers were and what activities they were involved in.

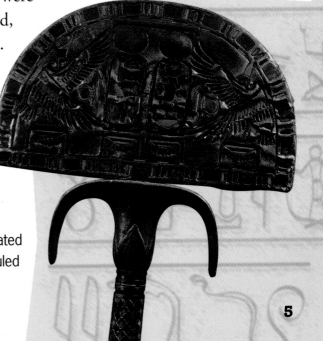

At one time this fan had feathers. It is decorated with the names of King Tutankhamen, who ruled Egypt around 1325 B.C.E.

Simple Hieroglyphic Signs

The oldest Egyptian **hieroglyphs** are called **ideograms.** These can be divided into two types: signs that stand for the objects they picture, and signs whose meanings are related in some basic way to what is being shown. An example of the first kind of ideogram is ⌣ , a picture of a mouth that stands for the word *mouth.* An example of the second kind is the symbol ⚖ , a picture of legs and feet walking. This hieroglyph stands for *motion.*

Ideograms are often seen with one stroke underneath them, like this: ⌷ . The stroke shows that this ideogram stands for the object it represents: a house. The same symbol without the stroke has a different meaning.

As hieroglyphic writing developed, Egyptians began to use ideograms without the stroke underneath to indicate certain sounds. These signs are called **phonograms.** They are similar to the letters used in English.

vulture **a**	foot **b**	basket with handle **c** or **k**	hand **d**	2 flowering reeds **e** or **y**	horned viper **f**
jar stand **g**	courtyard **h**	flowering reed **i**	snake **j**	basket with handle **k** or **c**	lion **l**
owl **m**	water **n**	lasso **o**	stool **p**	hill **q**	mouth **r**
folded cloth **s**	loaf **t**	quail chick **u**	horned viper **v**	coil of rope **w**	basket and cloth **x**
2 flowering reeds **y** or **e**	door bolt **z**	female	male	**KEY** hieroglyph ideogram phonogram	

In English, each letter stands for a particular sound, and the combination of sounds makes up a word. The Egyptian language had 24 of these single-sound hieroglyphs, while the English alphabet has 26 letters. This is because the sounds of the two languages are very different. Another difference between English and Egyptian is that vowel sounds (such as *a, e, i, o,* and *u)* were not written down in Egyptian. Because of this, we do not know exactly how the language of ancient Egypt was pronounced. People who want to read hieroglyphs out loud should just put an *e* sound between the consonants.

You can use the signs on the chart on page six to write your name or to write messages in hieroglyphs. Here are some examples:

Sam

Maria

Ryan

Make a Rebus Using Ideograms

As the Egyptian language and **script** developed, ideograms—signs that look like what they stand for—were used to represent words that had the same sound but a different meaning. An example of this in English would be: an ideogram of a fly being used to represent the action flying. This made it possible for the Egyptians to write words that could not be represented by a simple picture. A **rebus** uses ideograms in this way to communicate an idea. An example of a rebus in English would be:

This rebus means "I saw the bee fly to the flower." Here, the signs for bee and flower represent objects, while the sign for saw represents not the tool, but the action of seeing.

How Hieroglyphs Were Written

These signs are arranged in columns. They are read from top to bottom, left to right. The clue that tells you to read from left to right is that the birds face left.

The hieroglyphs on this stone are written in both vertical columns and horizontal lines.

When ancient Egyptians read or wrote, they usually started on the right and went to the left—exactly the opposite of how you read and write. But they did not always do this. Sometimes **hieroglyphs** were written to be read from left to right. The reader can tell which way to go by looking at the signs that are in the form of animals or people. If they face right, the reader should start reading from the right. If they face left, the reader should start at the left and go to the right.

In fact, it is very common for the hieroglyphs to be written left to right, right to left, in vertical columns, and in horizontal lines—all in one place! This is because the hieroglyphic texts are most commonly used along with pictures of people. Just like in cartoons, the hieroglyphs tell who the people are and what they are saying. The hieroglyphs will face the same way as the person who is "saying" the text. If there are no pictures of people, then the hieroglyphs will usually be written in horizontal lines, from right to left.

The Egyptians also wanted the signs to be symmetrical and balanced. So, if they were putting an **inscription** around a window, the signs to the left of the window would face right, and those to the right of the window would face left. It is easy to figure it out once you know what clues to look for.

The walls, doorways, and columns of this temple are covered with hieroglyphs and pictures of the king and the gods. The hieroglyphs around the doorway face the door opening.

The Egyptians did not put spaces between words or sentences, and they did not use punctuation such as periods or commas. This can make hieroglyphs difficult to read. But with some practice, it becomes easier to pick up the clues that indicate where one word ends and another one starts.

As a matter of fact, the ancient Egyptians disliked any kind of blank space in their writing. In English, we put spaces between words and sentences, **indent** paragraphs, and use margins to make a page look balanced. But the Egyptians liked their hieroglyphic signs to run all together in a group. If they thought it would look better, they would sometimes write the hieroglyphs in blocks, putting signs next to or on top of one another to better fill the available space.

The first two columns of hieroglyphs on the left face the same way as the hawk-headed god. They describe who he is. The other six columns to the right are about the woman. They face the same way as she does.

9

Determinatives

Since the ancient Egyptians did not use punctuation or put spaces between sentences, how do **translators** know when one word or sentence ends and another begins? Often they can find out what makes sense by reading the **hieroglyphs.** Also, Egyptians sometimes used red ink to indicate the beginning of a new section.

Some Determinatives

Determinatives are placed at the end of a word, after the other signs. Below are some determinatives.

	foreign or hilly country
	temple
	boat

There is also another way translators can tell where ideas begin and end. Experienced translators can often tell when one word ends and another begins by finding signs called **determinatives.** These signs are placed after a word written in hieroglyphs. Determinatives give the reader clues to the meaning of the word. For example, the name for ancient Egypt used the sounds *kmt* (probably pronounced "Kemet"). This was written . To show that the word stands for a place, the determinative for *town*, , was placed after the signs that spelled out the name of the place. The people of ancient Egypt used determinatives like this to clarify the meaning of many words.

Determinatives give a general idea of the meaning of the word to which they are attached. However, they were also used to make a difference between words that sounded alike but had very different meanings. For example, three signs , or *hnw,* were used to spell several common words. Determinatives were used to tell the reader which word was being referred to.

Examples of how determinatives were used:

⬚ 〜〜 🧍🏺 refers to a kind of jar (note the little jar);

⬚ 〜〜 🧍🕺 means "to celebrate" (note the man gesturing);

⬚ 〜〜 🧍👤👤 means "neighbors" (with a man and woman).

Determinatives could also be used to give additional meaning to words. For example, 🖋, a picture of a pen case and an ink **palette,** is the hieroglyph for *scribe* or *writing*. To indicate a female scribe, a picture of a woman would be placed after the symbol: 🖋👤.

Signs for Multiple-Letter Sounds

In English, there are many two-letter sounds, such as *th, sp,* and *bl.* These sounds are written with two letters because the English language is made up entirely of letters that stand for a single sound.

In the ancient Egyptian language, however, there are many single hieroglyphs that stand for two or even three sounds put together!

Below are some common multiple-letter **phonograms:**

☐ *pr*   🔱 *nfr*

▽ *nb*   ▭ *mn*

Plurals and Pairs

Plurals are words that indicate more than one of something. In English, a plural is usually formed by adding "s" or "es" to the end of a word. For example, the word *house* is made plural by adding an "s" to the end to make *houses*. Ancient Egyptians could make words plural in several ways.

One way to form a plural with **hieroglyphs** was to put three lines after the word like this, III, or like this, ⦂ . For example, the hieroglyph for **scribe,** 𓏞𓀀 , is written 𓏞𓀀 III in the plural. But the three lines do not indicate that there were exactly three scribes. This was just a simple way of indicating *many.*

Also, if a word could be expressed with a single **ideogram,** it could be written three times to make a plural. For example, the hieroglyph for *house,* 𓉐 , could be written in the plural as 𓉐𓉐𓉐 .

This text is on the wall of the tomb of King Ramses VI, who ruled Egypt around 1140 B.C.E. The text is a prayer asking the gods for protection in the **afterlife.** There are many plural words here—look for the three strokes. The signs are read from left to right, top to bottom.

Another way to make a plural is to write the **determinative** three times. The hieroglyphs for *ruler,* 𓇓𓂦𓀁 , would be 𓇓𓂦𓀁𓀁𓀁 in the plural.

In the Egyptian language, *plural* meant "three or more." To indicate only two of something, ancient Egyptians used a special form called the **dual.** The dual could be written in three ways. For example, *two eyes* could be indicated by writing the ideogram twice: ∅ ∅ . The dual could also be shown by putting two strokes after the word like this: ∅ \\ . Finally, the dual could be indicated by writing the determinative twice.

How to Translate Hieroglyphs

There are several steps in the **translation** of hieroglyphs:

1) First, the sound values of the groups of hieroglyphs are determined. This is called transliteration. Transliteration indicates the individual words and where they start and stop.

2) Then each word is looked up in a hieroglyphic-English dictionary.

3) Finally, because the rules of grammar for the Egyptian language are different than in English, the words may have to be reorganized.

Below is an example of the translation process for a simple sentence:

	pr	nsw	n	pr	f
1)	pr	nsw	n	pr	f
2)	Goes	king	to	house	his
3)	The king goes to his house.				

Ancient Egyptian Scripts

Ancient Egyptians used three forms of writing. The first type is **hieroglyphic** writing. Hieroglyphs were primarily carved into the stone of **monuments,** temples, and tombs. However, Egyptians also wrote many letters, contracts, and records with a brush and ink. Because these documents had to be completed quickly, the Egyptians created a simpler form of writing.

This second type of writing, used from about 2500 B.C.E. to 650 B.C.E., is called **hieratic. Egyptologists** refer to hieratic as a cursive **script** based on hieroglyphs. Ancient Egyptians used hieratic writing for business and **administrative** records. Hieratic script was written and read only from right to left. Sometimes hieratic signs were joined in the same way letters are joined in English cursive writing.

The third type of script, also based on hieroglyphs, is called **demotic.** Around 650 B.C.E., it replaced hieratic as the main cursive script. It is even simpler than hieratic writing, and historians believe it was developed mainly for use in offices. The Egyptians used demotic script for about 700 years.

Types of Carving

The ancient Egyptians carved hieroglyphs and pictures in two ways. The first kind of carving is called sunk **relief.** The **artisans** who used this method carved deep lines into the stone. The other method is called raised relief. For this method, the artisans carved out the background so that what was left was a raised picture or hieroglyph.

The signs here are carved into the background. This is a sunk relief.

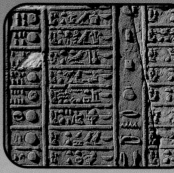

These signs stand out from the background. This is a raised relief.

While the hieratic and demotic forms of writing were quicker to write, they were not always easy to read. Some **paleographers** and Egyptologists convert hieratic and demotic script into hieroglyphs before **translating** a text into English. While the cursive forms became very common, hieroglyphs were still used in **inscriptions**.

Demotic texts were often written on a piece of broken pottery or a piece of stone. This one is a receipt for a purchase of land. Demotic script is very cursive and can be hard to read. It is always read from right to left.

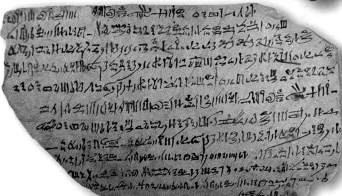

This hieratic text is written on a piece of stone. The **scribe's** handwriting is better than most! Egyptologists can date many hieratic texts by the style of handwriting.

Coptic

By about C.E. 350, the Egyptians began writing their language in a script called Coptic. Coptic is much easier to read and write than hieroglyphs, hieratic script, or demotic script. It has only 30 signs, and most of them are taken from the Greek alphabet. This was the simplest form of Egyptian writing, because all of the **determinatives** and most of the signs that stood for more than one sound were eliminated. Coptic is always written from left to right. It is still used in the Coptic (Egyptian Christian) Church.

This piece of pottery has a text in Coptic listing the twelve apostles. It was written around C.E. 600.

The Rosetta Stone

In 332 B.C.E., the **civilization** of ancient Egypt was taken over by Greek rulers. For the next 500 years, many people in Egypt used the Greek language and **script.** The Egyptian language was still used, but it was usually written in **demotic** script. The demotic script was replaced by Coptic around C.E. 350. Coptic was based on the Greek alphabet with a few Egyptian characters added. When Arab invaders took over in about C.E. 640, most Egyptians adopted the Arabic language.

The Rosetta Stone is a little less than four feet (1.2 meters) high. The text is from the time of **Pharaoh** Ptolemy V.

For thousands of years, no one could read the strange signs that survived on many Egyptian **monuments.** The **hieroglyphs** were like a secret code that could not be understood because no one held the key.

That all changed in 1798 when the French military leader Napoleon led his troops to Egypt. While a group of soldiers was rebuilding a fort in the town of Rosetta (called Rashid in Egypt), one of the men found a black stone that had many symbols carved into it. It was clear that there were three types of writing on the stone. But the man recognized only one of them: Greek.

Later, it was determined that the other two kinds of writing on the stone were hieroglyphic script and demotic script. These three scripts were carved into the stone because they were being used in Egypt when the stone was carved. The stone was carved near the end of ancient Egyptian civilization, when Greek rulers had taken over. The rulers would have read the Greek script on the Rosetta Stone. The script used by common people was demotic. Hieroglyphs were used mainly by priests in the temples.

The text on the Rosetta Stone includes the command that it be written in Greek, demotic script, and hieroglyphs so that everyone would be able to read it. The text is about the restoration of temples during the reign of King Ptolemy V. The date of the text corresponds to March 27 of the year C.E. 196.

Historians were excited about the discovery. The Greek writing on the stone told them that all three passages said the same thing. They knew that they could use the Greek writing as a kind of key to figure out what the other texts said. If historians could figure out how to read hieroglyphs, they would discover many things about ancient Egypt!

Jean-Francois Champollion worked for several years to decipher the text on the Rosetta Stone. His success in translating the hieroglyphic and demotic signs opened the door to many new discoveries about the civilization of ancient Egypt.

Several scholars quickly began to work on **translating** the stone. They made some small discoveries, but not much real progress. Finally, a British scientist named Thomas Young was able to **decipher** a part of the writing. Some of his guesses were right, but he also made several errors that kept him from figuring out much more. When Young could go no further, another man, Jean-Francois Champollion, began trying to translate the stone. Champollion knew a great deal about ancient languages. In 1822, he made important discoveries that put him on the right track. By the time of his death ten years later, he had deciphered large sections of the hieroglyphic and demotic writing on the stone. It is because of his hard work that we now understand hieroglyphs.

The Names of the Gods

During the long period of time that their **civilization** existed, the ancient Egyptians worshiped thousands of gods. But for most of that time, a few gods remained supreme.

One of the most important gods was the sun god, Re (also sometimes spelled "Ra" and pronounced *RAH).* He crossed the sky every day. When the sun set and disappeared at night, the Egyptians thought Re passed into the **underworld.** Every morning, he came back to life. The **hieroglyphic** name for Re is ⌇⊙ or ⊙𓀀 .

The god Re is shown as a man with a hawk head and a sun disk. The round sun disk itself is the hieroglyph for *Re.*

Osiris was another important god. He was killed by his brother Seth and was forced to live in the underworld. Re visited Osiris every night as he passed through the underworld. Osiris was also said to judge people's souls after they died. The hieroglyphic name for Osiris is 𓊨𓁹 or 𓁹𓊨 .

Khepri was the god of the morning sun. He is pictured as a **scarab** beetle, and that is also part of his hieroglyphic sign: 𓆣𓏤𓇳 . He is shown in paintings as an entire beetle or as a man with the head of a beetle.

Khepri is represented by a scarab beetle. Here the scarab is pushing the sun into the sky at dawn.

Isis was an important goddess. She represented the ideal wife and mother. Isis was also the protector of the dead. Her sign is 𓊨𓏏𓁐 .

This statue of Horus shows him wearing a royal crown because he was so closely linked to the pharaoh.

The son of Osiris and Isis was Horus, the god of the sky. Horus appears as a falcon or a hawk, and is often called the falcon-god. Ancient Egyptians believed that the **pharaoh,** their ruler, was Horus in human form. When the pharaoh died, he became Osiris. The new ruler became the new Horus. The hieroglyph for the god Horus looks like this: 𓅃 .

Anubis is seen in the art of many tombs where important ancient Egyptians were buried. He is often shown with a man's body and a **jackal's** head. He is also shown simply as a jackal. Anubis was the god of **embalming** and held the keys to the underworld. The hieroglyphic sign for the god Anubis is 𓇋𓐍𓃢 or 𓃣 .

The general hieroglyph for *god* is 𓊹 . Hieroglyphs for gods were so important that they were always placed in front of all other signs, no matter where they were actually to be read in the text. For example, in the phrase *servant of god,* the hieroglyph for *god* was placed before the sign for *servant,* even though the words are said in the opposite order.

Isis is usually shown with a tall headdress of cow horns and a sun disk.

The god Anubis had the head of a jackal because these animals roamed the graveyards at night.

Monuments to Gods and Kings

The gods the Egyptians worshiped were central to their everyday lives. Ancient Egyptians praised the gods in the letters they wrote and in the greetings they said to their friends as they passed on the street. The Egyptians thought that their rulers were earthly forms of gods who would become gods when they died. For this reason, the **monuments** built to honor them were grand and majestic, as were the messages written on them.

Beginning in the early years of their **civilization**—about 2700 B.C.E.—the ancient Egyptians built **pyramids.** These huge structures were tombs for kings. The three best-known pyramids are those at Giza, but pyramids have been found at many sites in Egypt, and **archaeologists** still hope to discover more. Inside the pyramids are tombs. On the walls of some of the tombs are thousands of **hieroglyphs.** These messages help guide the dead through the **underworld** and into the **afterlife.**

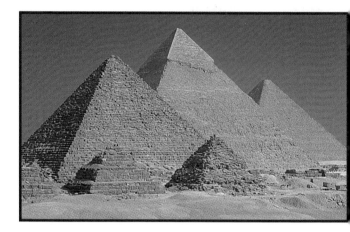

The pyramids at Giza are enormous structures that were built about 4,500 years ago. The pyramids are burial chambers for pharaohs, their families, and their close **advisors.**

This is the inside of the tomb of King Ramses VI. The walls are covered in paintings and hieroglyphs.

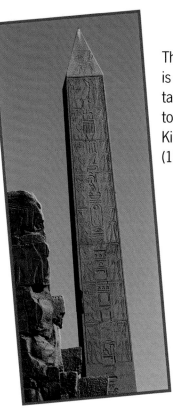

The obelisk at Karnak is 75 feet (23 meters) tall and weighs 143 tons. It was built by King Thutmose I (1505 B.C.E.).

The temple of Ramses II at Abu Simbel has four statues of the king.

Each statue at Abu Simbel has the **cartouche** of Ramses II on its arm.

Egyptologists can only guess at how the Egyptians built the pyramids. They think it took about 20,000 people and many years to complete them. The workers might have built mud-covered ramps on which they could pull up the huge stones. If so, the ramps might have been kept wet so that they were slippery. Then the workers would have tied thick ropes around the stones and dragged them up the ramps.

Another kind of ancient Egyptian monument is the **obelisk**. This is a tall pillar with four sides that come to a pyramid-shaped point at the top. The Washington Monument in Washington, D.C. is a good example of an obelisk in the United States. In ancient Egypt, obelisks were covered with hieroglyphs. The obelisks were placed at the entrances to temples. Some people believe that obelisks were designed to represent rays of the sun.

The Egyptians built many large temples to honor their gods and kings. One famous temple was built by the **pharaoh** Ramses II, who ruled from 1279 to 1213 B.C.E. The temple, called Abu Simbel, is built into the side of a mountain.

The Journey of the Dead

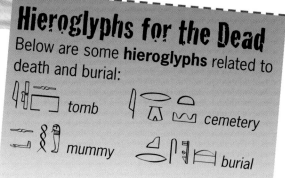

Hieroglyphs for the Dead

Below are some **hieroglyphs** related to death and burial:

tomb   cemetery   mummy   burial

When many people think of ancient Egypt, they think of mummies. That is not surprising, since the ancient Egyptians made thousands of mummies, and many of them are still around today. But why did ancient Egyptians **mummify** the bodies of the dead?

The answer lies in the ancient Egyptians' beliefs about what happened to a person after he or she died. They believed that after death, a person first went on a journey through the **underworld.** Once a person passed through the underworld, the Egyptians believed that he or she went to a life much like the one on Earth. This life was called the **afterlife.** They believed that the dead would need their bodies in the afterlife. Therefore, they mummified bodies to preserve them.

This is the tomb of a man named Sennedjem, a professional artist. It is decorated with scenes from *The Book of the Dead.*

At many points during the journey through the underworld, **gatekeepers** would ask the dead person questions. The dead person had to remember all of the answers and respond to the questions correctly. If they did so, the gatekeepers would clear the person's path by opening a gate or allowing him or her to cross a river.

This page from *The Book of the Dead* shows four gods in the form of mummies. They protected the body in the afterlife.

A dead person also encountered dangerous demons during the journey through the underworld. The demons would back down only if they were addressed by name. The dead person had to know who they were and remember their names.

Special spells also could be spoken to get rid of the dangerous creatures in the underworld. There were so many spells that people were afraid they could not remember them all. To help a dead person, his or her family would have an artist write the spells on the walls of the tomb or on a sheet of **papyrus.** By about 1550 B.C.E., a book was written to help dead people on their journey through the underworld. The book was called *Coming Forth by Day,* but today we know it more simply as *The Book of the Dead.* This collection of spells was often put into a tomb so the dead person could use it on his or her journey.

Words for the Dead

The passage to the **afterlife** was considered to be dangerous, so many prayers and spells protected the dead person. Some of these were written on the walls of the tomb, or they were written on **papyrus** paper and buried with the **mummy.** Other spells were spoken by priests at the funeral.

The Speech of Isis

The Book of the Dead is made up of many spells that called upon the gods to protect the soul of the dead in the afterlife. One part of the book is a speech by the goddess Isis. She restores the windpipe of the dead person so he or she can breathe freely. Isis also brings fresh air into the tomb. She promises to protect the dead from his or her enemies on the journey through the **underworld.** She says:

> I have come to be your protection. I give air to your nostrils, and the north wind that comes from the god Atum to your nose. I have made your windpipe whole. I make you live as a god. Your enemies shall be at your feet. I have made your word true before goddess Nut. You are mighty before the gods!

A dead person's stomach, liver, lungs, and intestines were removed to keep the body from decaying. Because the dead person needed the organs in the afterlife, they were dried and stored in jars like these.

Scarabs

In Egyptian art, the god Khepri was drawn as a kind of beetle called a **scarab.** The scarab is also a **hieroglyph** that means "to come into being." A scarab made of stone was placed close to the mummy's heart. Egyptians believed the heart was like the soul or even the brain. A spell from *The Book of the Dead* was carved on the back side of the stone scarab. The spell tells the heart not to tell lies about the dead person during the final judgment by the gods. In this judgement, the heart was put on a balance scale and weighed against the feather of truth. This was how the gods could see if the person had lived a good or a bad life. If the test proved that the dead person was good, he or she would be reborn in the afterlife. Part of the scarab text says:

This scarab with wings is from the tomb of King Tutankhamen.

Spell for not letting the heart judge against him. Oh heart from my mother! Do not stand up against me as a witness. Do not oppose me at the judgement...Do not make my name stink to the judges. It will be good for me...that the judge may be happy. Do not make up lies about me before the judge.

In this scene from *The Book of the Dead*, the god Anubis is weighing the heart of a dead person in the judgement hall of Osiris. On the other side of the scale is the feather of truth.

Special Symbols

The key to the temple at Abu Simbel is in the form of a large *ankh*. The ancient Egyptians used the *ankh* on jewelry and many other objects.

Some **hieroglyphs** were symbols for things that were important to the people of ancient Egypt. They were often used in pictures and in other **artifacts,** such as jewelry.

One special hieroglyph is the *ankh,* ♀ . This hieroglyphic symbol means "life" or "to live." It appears often in paintings and hieroglyphic carvings on tomb walls because of the strong Egyptian belief in life after death. The symbol is often held by a god, and sometimes the god offers the *ankh* to a **pharaoh.**

Another special symbol is the *shen* sign, ☿ . It means "eternity."

The goddess Nekhbet, shown here as a bird, holds a *shen* sign over the ruler's head. This means that she gives the king eternal rule.

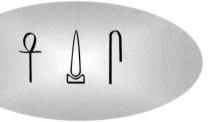

These three symbols were often used as greetings in letters. They stand for life, prosperity, and health.

The lotus flower, held by the figure on the left, is a symbol of the Sun, creation, and rebirth. Lotus flowers grew along the banks of the Nile River.

The Wedjat Eye

The **wedjat eye** is the eye of Horus. One story says that Horus lost the eye in a fight with his uncle Seth, who tore it out and ripped it apart. Then Thoth, the god of wisdom and the moon, made the eye whole again and returned it to Horus. The eye was supposed to keep evil spirits away and help the dead as they made their journey through the **underworld.** It symbolizes healing, wholeness, and victory over evil.

The Names of the Kings

The Egyptians thought that their **pharaoh**—as the king was called after about 1554 B.C.E.—was a god on Earth. The pharaoh was thought to be Horus in human form. The people of ancient Egypt honored their ruler in many ways, including the way they wrote his name.

By about 2450 B.C.E., each pharaoh had five names. The first three names indicated the king's role as a god, while the last two indicated his or her role as a person and ruler.

The first name, which showed that the pharaoh was a god in human form, was the Horus-name. It was written with a falcon (the **hieroglyph** for the god Horus) followed by a rectangle called a *serekh*. The *serekh* represents the pharaoh's palace. The pharaoh's name was written inside the *serekh*. The Horus-name was the earliest form of a pharaoh's name. In the early part of Egyptian history, until about 3000 B.C.E., it was the only name that pharaohs had.

The second name is called the Two Ladies. At one time, Egypt may have been divided into two parts: Upper (southern) and Lower (northern) Egypt. Each area had its own patron goddess: Nekhbet (a vulture) in Upper Egypt, and Wadjet (a snake) in Lower Egypt. The second name gave the king the protection of these two goddesses. The third name is the Golden Horus name. It associates the king with the power of Horus.

One of the earliest historical records from Egypt is this slab of stone showing King Narmer. Here Narmer is defeating his northern enemies to unify Egypt. Narmer's Horus-name, a chisel and a catfish, is in the *serekh* at the top.

The fourth name, called the **prenomen,** follows the title "King of Upper and Lower Egypt." A pharaoh received this name when he came into power. Texts indicate that priests made up the name for the coronation ceremony. Almost all prenomens include the name of the sun god Re, showing the love of the king for that god. This name is written in an oval **cartouche.**

The final name, or **nomen,** is the name that the pharaoh had before he became king. It is like a family name. It is also enclosed in a cartouche. It follows a title, "Son of Re," which means that the pharaoh was the son of the sun god. All together, these five names and titles are called the **royal titulary.**

What Is a Cartouche?

Beginning around 2600 B.C.E., the name of the ruler of ancient Egypt was written in an oval called a cartouche. The cartouche represents a loop of rope tied at one end. The Egyptians called the cartouche *shen,* which means "that which [the sun] closes." Putting the royal name in the loop meant that the king ruled all that the sun shone upon. The word *cartouche* comes from the French word for an oval bullet or gun cartridge.

This cartouche encloses the name of King Teti, who ruled about 2400 B.C.E. The title "Son of Re" is also inside this cartouche.

Telling Stories

Many of the paintings and **hieroglyphs** on tomb walls present stories or events from everyday life. Some of them show events that the Egyptians expected to happen in the **underworld** and the **afterlife.** Other tomb decorations tell stories of what the dead person did while alive.

The paintings provide a lot of information about the lives of ancient Egyptians—what they wore, their hairstyles, what kind of work they did, and the games they played. Most of these paintings have hieroglyphic texts near them that explain exactly what is happening and who the people are.

This scene of female musicians is from the tomb of the nobleman Nakht, who lived around 1352 B.C.E. The painting would ensure that Nakht had music in the afterlife.

In this painting, the nobleman Nakht is hunting birds from a boat. The hieroglyphs explain what Nakht is doing. Since birds can symbolize disorder, the scene also means that Nakht is conquering evil.

The paintings in the tombs are very beautiful, but they are not always truthful. Egyptian artists showed only the best side of life because that is what they wanted to preserve for eternity. Notice in the paintings shown here that all the people are slender, healthy, and well-dressed. We know from ancient writings that there was sickness and poverty in ancient Egypt. However, these things are never shown in tomb paintings.

This painting from the tomb of an artist shows him and his wife cutting **flax,** the plant used to make **linen.** They would have never actually done this kind of work in their lifetime—and certainly not wearing such fine clothes!

Animals

Most hieroglyphs are in the form of things that the Egyptians saw around them. Hundreds of signs are in the form of animals. More than 50 common hieroglyphs are of birds alone! Some of these hieroglyphs are **ideograms,** some are **phonograms,** and some are **determinatives.**

 hare, phonogram for the sound *wn*

 frog, phonogram for the sound *hfn*

 owl, phonogram for the sound *m*

 scarab beetle, phonogram for the sound *hpr*

 cobra, phonogram for the *dj* sound

 fish, determinative for *fish*

 dog, determinative for *dog*

Keeping Records

The people of ancient Egypt kept many records. They recorded how many animals and prisoners they had captured during a war, how much livestock they owned, and how many offerings were presented to a particular god. They also kept lists of what supplies were kept in temples and warehouses. They collected taxes each year and kept lists of who paid, when they paid, and how much they paid. The possessions of dead people were listed on their tomb walls so they could take everything with them in the **afterlife.**

Except for the lists on tomb and temple walls, most records were written in **hieratic** or **demotic script** on long rolls of **papyrus** paper and leather. The records were rolled up and kept in stacks. They were labeled so that people who needed them could find them easily.

This text is about King Seti II, who ruled around 1199 B.C.E. It tells of **monuments** that the king built for the god Amun.

This piece of stone from the tomb of Prince Ra-hotep shows him seated at an offering table. The closely spaced hieroglyphs to the right are a list of the objects he wanted in the afterlife.

The **cartouches** on this wall represent the names of kings who ruled in ancient Egypt until about 1280 B.C.E.

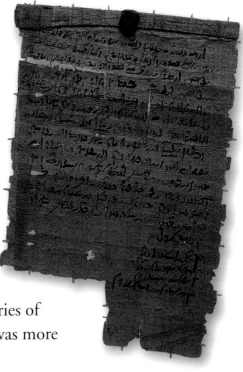

This is a record of a loan of grain and the amount to be paid. It is written on papyrus in demotic script.

Records were also kept on large pieces, or slabs, of stone. Some of these were placed at the entrances of tombs and listed the names of the people who were buried inside. The Egyptians also recorded stories of battles or wars on slabs of stone. This information was more likely to be **inscribed** with **hieroglyphs.**

The Egyptian Number System

The ancient Egyptians used a number system based on the number ten, like the system of numbering used today. They grouped numbers into tens and used separate hieroglyphs for *1, 10, 100, 1,000,* and so on. The symbol for the number appeared as many times as necessary to show the amount.

For example, to express the number *60,* they would write the hieroglyph for *10* six times, like this: ∩ ∩ ∩ ∩ ∩ ∩ .

Signs for higher numbers were put in front of signs for lower numbers, so *324* would look like this: ℗℗℗∩∩IIII .

Below are some Egyptian hieroglyphs for numbers:

1 | 10 ∩   100 ℗   1000 𓆼

Can you figure out these numbers? The answers are on page 47.

𓆼℗℗| ∩∩||| ℗℗℗∩|

Scribes

Scribes went to special schools to learn how to write the Egyptian language in **hieratic** and **hieroglyphic scripts.** The position of the scribe was highly valued in ancient Egypt. Scribes were called *sesh* in the Egyptian language. The autobiographical text of one scribe says that he started school when he was five years old, attended for four years, and then worked as an apprentice for another eleven years. Scribes were almost always men. Although some girls learned to write, they studied at home.

In scribe school, students learned hieratic writing first. Their teachers, called *sebai,* wrote the texts on a **whitewashed** board. Student scribes copied the texts onto small pieces of pottery or stone. Sometimes they would write on **papyrus** paper, but it was considered too valuable for everyday use.

This statue shows an ancient Egyptian scribe. Scribes are often shown sitting in this position, with an unrolled sheet of papyrus over the lap.

Once a student had learned hieratic script, he went on to learn hieroglyphs. When the student had finally learned the approximately 800 hieroglyphs to the satisfaction of his teacher, he was allowed to get a job. Most graduates became clerks and recorders—people who kept records for the government. They were often promoted to become priests, government officials, and military leaders. A few scribes even became kings!

Student scribes spent hours copying texts. Many of the texts they copied taught a moral lesson. Advanced students also copied sample letters like the ones they would copy once they finished school and got a job. Teachers in ancient Egypt used red ink to correct their students' mistakes.

A group of scribes writes down the amounts of grain that have been brought from the fields. Each holds a pen box that also contains an ink supply. Scribes were an important part of the government because they kept track of everything.

Life of a Scribe

The ancient Egyptians had great respect for scribes. They also thought it was one of the best, and easiest, professions. One text from about 1200 B.C.E. compares different jobs. It says that the blacksmith works at his furnace, with fingers that look like the claws of a crocodile. The gardener carries a yoke and works himself to death. The fisherman has the worst job because he works close to crocodiles. The text continues, saying that a scribe has the best job:

There is no profession without a boss except for the scribe. He is the boss. If you know writing, it will be better for you than any other profession. Set your heart on books! There is nothing better than books.

Tools

The **hieroglyph** for *scribe,* 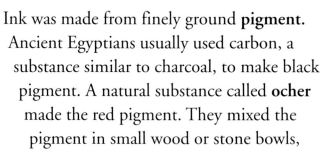, contains some of a scribe's most important tools, including a **palette,** pen case, and bag. The tools are connected by a string or leather strap. Drawings found in ancient Egypt show that scribes often carried these items by putting the string or strap over one shoulder.

The palette was usually made of wood and shaped like a rectangle. In the center was a long groove where the scribe could store his pens. Most palettes also had two round areas. One contained a cake of black ink and the other red ink.

The pens used by scribes were made from plants called reeds that grew along the Nile River. Scribes made one end into a fine brush by chewing and sucking it until it became soft. After the scribe had used the brush for a while, he had to cut off the worn end and start the process over to make a new brush. Scribes could also use larger, hollow reeds that they cut at a sharp angle. This made a finer line, like a modern fountain pen.

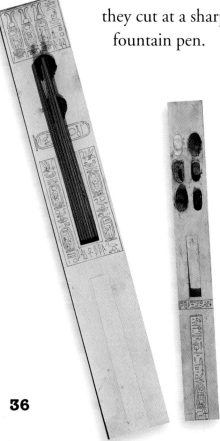

Ink was made from finely ground **pigment.** Ancient Egyptians usually used carbon, a substance similar to charcoal, to make black pigment. A natural substance called **ocher** made the red pigment. They mixed the pigment in small wood or stone bowls,

This picture shows two kinds of palettes. Both have a space for reed pens. The larger palette has cakes of red and black ink. The smaller palette has additional colors used for decorating papyrus paper.

The scribe on the left is writing a list of what is in the boxes in front of him. His pen case is resting on his knee, and extra brushes are stuck behind his ear.

adding a substance with a texture like chewing gum that they got from several different plants. Then they formed the ink into round cakes and let the cakes dry. When the scribes needed to use the ink, they dipped a brush into water and rubbed the wet brush on a dry cake of ink. This is how watercolors are used today.

Scribes also used small containers of water to dip their pens into. To sharpen and cut their pens, they used pieces of sharp stone. They could also use these to cut sheets of **papyrus** to the size that they needed.

Two scribes are shown sitting in a room with tall pillars. The hieroglyphs give their names and lists their job.

Papyrus

The ancient Egyptians made a material called **papyrus.** This was the earliest known kind of paper. Papyrus was named after the plant it was made from. The papyrus plant is a long reed that grew—and still grows—along the banks of the Nile River.

After the Egyptians collected the papyrus reeds, they peeled them and cut them into long, thin strips. They laid out some of the strips next to each other to form a layer and then laid a second layer crosswise on the top. Then they put a sheet of **linen** over the layers and either put heavy rocks on the layers or pounded the layers with a **mallet.** The pounding made the sap come out of the plant. The sticky sap made the layers of papyrus reed stick together. Finally, the sap was allowed to dry.

Even though papyrus paper is made of strong fibers, it is smooth and flat. Rolls of papyrus could be made as long as 35 feet (11 meters) or more. It was popular in its day—in fact, the Egyptians even traded it to other countries.

Papyrus paper was hard to make and expensive, so it was used only for important writing such as official government records. **Scribes** used reed pens and ink to write on papyrus paper in **hieratic** or **demotic script.**

The papyrus plant was not used just for paper. In ancient Egypt, the stem of the plant was also used to make cloth, sandals, sails, baskets, and mats.

Papyrus Hieroglyphs

These are some **hieroglyphs** related to papyrus:

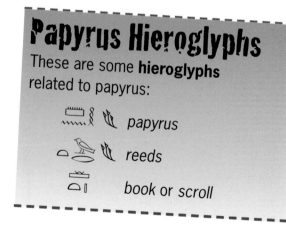

papyrus

reeds

book or scroll

Famous Ancient Papyrus

The Ebers Papyrus is one of the earliest known medical texts. It was written around 1550 B.C.E. and contains 700 magical formulas and cures. The papyrus is 110 pages long. It is written in hieratic script.

The Rhind Papyrus contains numerical tables as well as 84 mathematical problems and their solutions. It was copied in about 1650 B.C.E. by a scribe named Ahmes. The original text was written 200 years earlier. The papyrus is almost twenty feet (six meters) long. It is written in hieratic script.

The Turin Papyrus, or the *Turin Canon of Kings*, was written around 1300 B.C.E. It is a list of all the Egyptian kings, beginning in about 3000 B.C.E. It includes the names of the rulers as well as information about how long they ruled, down to the number of days. It even predicts who would rule the kingdom in the future. Today, the papyrus is kept in a museum in Turin, Italy. The papyrus is in pieces now, but it is important to historians because it provides a complete list of the kings who ruled Egypt for about 1,500 years.

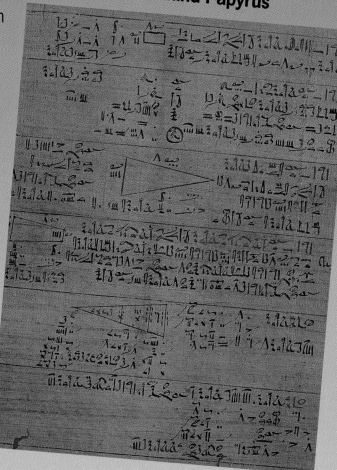

The Rhind Papyrus

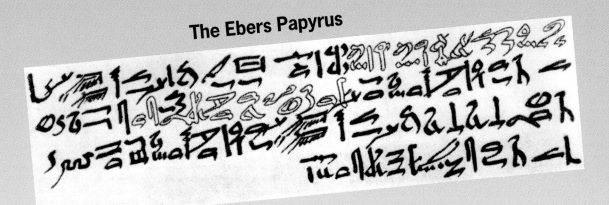

The Ebers Papyrus

Other Kinds of Hieroglyphic Writing

In addition to ancient Egypt, other **civilizations** used **hieroglyphic** writing. The Maya, for example, had a very complicated form of hieroglyphs. Their civilization lasted from about C.E. 250 to C.E. 900 in parts of Central America.

Mayan hieroglyphs look very different from Egyptian hieroglyphs.

Mayan hieroglyphs are very difficult to understand. For years, no one could read them. Then **archaeologists** found some ancient Mayan books that helped **epigraphers**—people who study **inscriptions**—to read some of the hieroglyphs. One reason the hieroglyphs are so difficult to **translate** is that a symbol could stand for a word, part of a word, or an idea. And the symbols can be read from left to right, right to left, top to bottom, or bottom to top.

Another ancient civilization that used hieroglyphic writing was the Hittites, who lived in what is now Turkey. They developed their system in about 1500 B.C.E., well after the Egyptians began using hieroglyphs. Some symbols represented complete words, while others stood for sounds.

Hittite hieroglyphs change direction every row. Here, the top and bottom lines are read left to right, and the middle line is read right to left.

Interested in Being an Egyptologist?

Hieroglyphic writing is no longer used for communication, but people still study the signs and their meanings. Every year, archaeologists make new discoveries in Egypt. Epigraphers and **paleographers** study the writing they find. **Egyptologists** try to put it all together. All these people are historians, but each profession deals with something different.

Archaeologists need a good background in history, geography, science, mathematics, and languages—nearly every subject! In college, they usually study **anthropology.** Then they specialize in a particular area, such as the archaeology of ancient Egypt or ancient Greece. Underwater or marine archaeologists study shipwrecks at the bottom of the ocean. Archaeologists study the objects related to particular **cultures,** such as pottery, weapons, homes, and even the bones of dead people. Archaeologists examine these things to find out how the people lived and died.

Epigraphers study writing that has been cut into something solid and permanent, such as stone. Paleographers study all kinds of ancient writing. Epigraphers and paleographers study history, geography, languages, and anthropology. Many of them are also archaeologists.

Egyptologists concentrate on ancient Egypt. They study ancient Egyptian language, including hieroglyphs, **hieratic script, demotic** script, and Coptic script. They also learn about Egypt's history, including the gods and goddesses, the kings and queens, and the buildings and towns of ancient Egypt. They study how **mummies** were made and buried. They learn about the sites of the major tombs. To prepare, Egyptologists take many history and geography classes. They usually work in museums and universities, where they are often expected to do a lot of writing.

Archaeologists spend a lot of time digging for **artifacts.** They keep records of where the artifacts were found, what they look like, and what condition they are in. Some archaeologists spend all their time putting together broken artifacts or making sure they are preserved.

Timeline of Ancient Egypt

The history of ancient Egypt is divided into dynasties. A dynasty is a series of rulers, usually from the same family. The list continues up to the 31st dynasty, when the Romans took over Egypt in 30 B.C.E. The dynasties are grouped into five major periods: the Early Dynastic Period (3100 to 2755 B.C.E.), the Old Kingdom (2686 to 2181 B.C.E.), the Middle Kingdom (1991 to 1786 B.C.E.), the New Kingdom (1550 to 1070 B.C.E.), and the Late Period (664 to 525 B.C.E.). Some other dynasties had control of Egypt between, during, and after these periods.

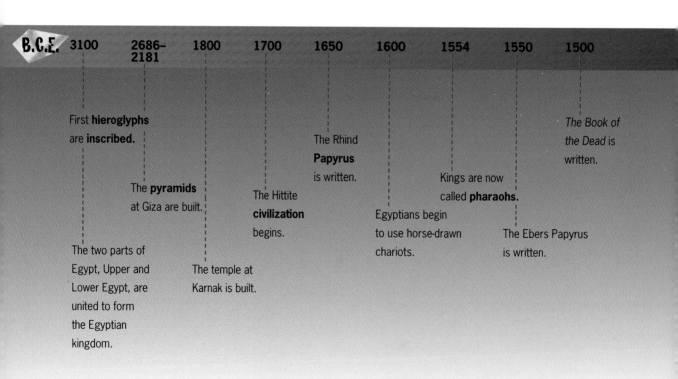

B.C.E. | 3100 | 2686–2181 | 1800 | 1700 | 1650 | 1600 | 1554 | 1550 | 1500

First **hieroglyphs** are **inscribed.**

The **pyramids** at Giza are built.

The Hittite **civilization** begins.

The Rhind **Papyrus** is written.

Egyptians begin to use horse-drawn chariots.

Kings are now called **pharaohs.**

The Ebers Papyrus is written.

The Book of the Dead is written.

The two parts of Egypt, Upper and Lower Egypt, are united to form the Egyptian kingdom.

The temple at Karnak is built.

Trees and crops could only be grown along the banks of the Nile River. This is where people built towns. Beyond that area was the desert. Generally, tombs were located in the deserts, away from the cities.

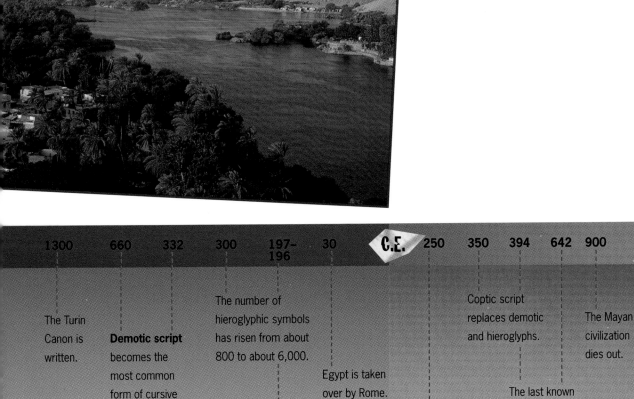

1300	660	332	300	197–196	30	C.E.	250	350	394	642	900

The Turin Canon is written.

Demotic script becomes the most common form of cursive writing.

The number of hieroglyphic symbols has risen from about 800 to about 6,000.

Egypt is taken over by Rome.

Coptic script replaces demotic and hieroglyphs.

The Mayan civilization dies out.

The last known hieroglyphs are carved into a stone on the island of Philae.

Egypt becomes part of the Macedonian empire and the city of Alexandria is founded.

The Rosetta Stone is inscribed with writing in Greek, hieroglyphs, and demotic script.

The Mayan civilization begins in Central America and southern Mexico.

Muslims from Arabia take control of Egypt.

Glossary

administrative related to the management of something, such as a government office or business

advisor person who gives help or advice

afterlife destination of the dead; for ancient Egyptians, a realm thought to be much like life here on Earth

anthropology science that studies human beings and their culture

archaeologist (ar-kee-AHL-oh-jist) person who studies the remains of past cultures, including bones and pottery

artifact something made by human skill or work, such as pottery, weapons, or clothing

artisan person who specializes in a particular craft

cartouche (car-TOOSH) long, oval shape that contains a pharaoh's name written in hieroglyphs

civilization way of life specific to a particular time and place

culture beliefs and customs of a group of people

decipher (dee-SIGH-fer) figure out a language or code using a key or other method

demotic (dee-MOT-ick) very cursive script used to write Egyptian language from about 650 B.C.E. to C.E. 350

determinative sign put after a word written in hieroglyphs that explains the meaning of the word

dual in ancient Egyptian language, a way of expressing two of something

Egyptologist person who specializes in the study of ancient Egypt

embalm preserve the body of a dead person

epigrapher (eh-PIG-ra-fer) person who studies writings carved into something hard, such as stone

flax plant with a strong fiber that is spun and made into linen

gatekeeper someone placed in front of an entrance or path who allows only certain people through.

hieratic (hi-er-AT-ick) simplified, cursive form of hieroglyphic writing used for business and government records

hieroglyph (HI-er-oh-glif) symbol or sign in a writing system that uses pictures to communicate ideas

ideogram (I-DEE-oh-gram) hieroglyph that stands for the object or action it pictures

indent make a space before beginning a new paragraph

inscription words carved into or written on something hard such as stone

jackal small wild dog that lives in Asia, Africa, and parts of Europe

linen light cloth made from the flax plant

mallet hammer with a large, heavy wooden head

monument large object such as a statue, pillar, or building, usually built in memory of a person or event

mummify make a dead body into a mummy by drying and preparing it

nomen fifth and final name of a pharaoh, given at birth

obelisk (OB-eh-lisk) tall stone pillar with a pyramid shape at the top

ocher (OH-ker) mixture of clay and iron oxide. Paint made from ocher ranges in color from pale yellow to reddish brown.

paleographer (pay-lee-AHG-ruh-fer) person who studies ancient writing on manuscripts, such as papyrus

palette (PAL-et) rectangular piece of wood used by scribes to hold pens and ink

papyrus (puh-PIE-rus) reedy plant that grows near the Nile River. Ancient Egyptians used papyrus to make papyrus paper as well as sails, boats, floor mats, and other items.

pharaoh (FAIR-oh) ancient Egyptian word that means "great house." The king of Egypt was called pharaoh starting around 1550 B.C.E.

phonogram hieroglyph that represents a sound in the language of ancient Egypt

pigment powder used to color paints and inks. Pigment comes from plants and sometimes animals.

prenomen fourth name of a pharaoh, given when he comes into power

pyramid four-sided monument that comes to a point at the top

rebus word game that uses pictures to represent words

relief sculpture in which either the background or the picture is carved away

royal titulary (TITCH-uh-LAIR-ee) group of five names of a pharaoh

scarab (SCARE-ub) type of beetle. The hieroglyph picturing a scarab means "to come into being." Scarabs were used in jewelry and other types of decoration.

scribe person specially trained in reading and writing

script any kind of handwriting

translate change one language into another. A person who does this, either on paper or speaking, is called a translator.

underworld dangerous place the dead had to travel through to reach the afterlife

wedjat eye eye that Horus lost in a fight with the god Seth; restored by the god Thoth. Ancient Egyptians used the symbol of the eye to keep evil spirits away.

whitewash paint used to make a surface appear white

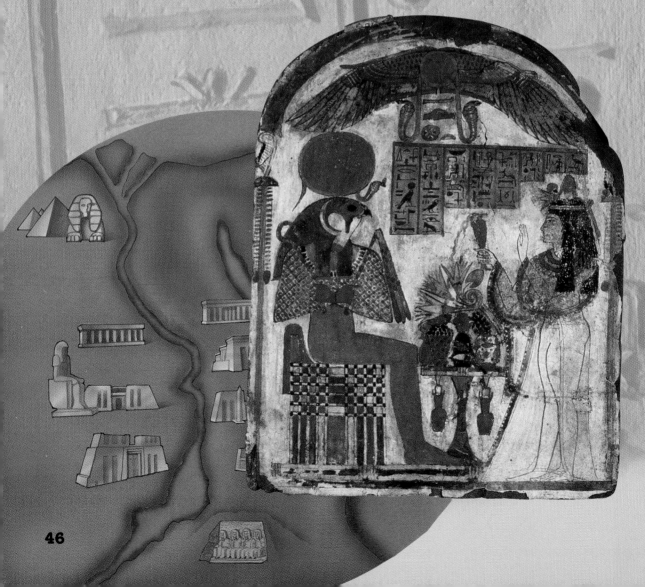

More Books to Read

Armentrout, David and Patricia Armentrout. *Treasures from Egypt.* Vero Beach, Fla.: Rourke Book Company, Inc., 2001.

Coulter, Laurie. *Secrets in Stone: All About Maya Hieroglyphics.* New York: Little, Brown, & Company, 2001.

Donoughue, Carol. *The Mystery of Hieroglyphs: The Story of the Rosetta Stone and the Race to Decipher Egyptian Hieroglyphs.* New York: Oxford University Press, 1999.

Milton, Joyce. *Hieroglyphs.* New York: Grosset & Dunlap, 2000.

Shuter, Jane. *Ancient Egypt.* Austin, Tex.; Raintree Steck-Vaughn, 2000.

Places to Visit

The Metropolitan Museum of Art
1000 Fifth Avenue at 82nd Street
New York, NY 10028
Visitor information: (212) 535-7710

The Museum of Fine Arts, Houston
1001 Bissonnet Street
Houston, TX 77005
Visitor information: (713) 639-7300

The Oriental Institute Museum
1155 East 58th Street
Chicago, IL 60637
Visitor information: (773) 702-9514

Carnegie Museum of Natural History
4400 Forbes Avenue
Pittsburgh, PA 15213
Visitor information: (412) 622-3131

Florida International Museum
100 Second Street North
St. Petersburg, FL 33701
Visitor information: (800) 777-9882

Seattle Art Museum
100 University Street
Seattle, WA 98101
Visitor Information: (206) 654-3100

Answers to Page 33:

2,001; 23; 211

Index